I0013369

AWS Certified

Solutions Architect – Associate

Study Guide & Exam Prep

Copyright © Black Chili Limited 2020. All rights reserved.

A catalogue record for this book is available from the British Library.

ISBN: 978-1-911064-11-4

No part of this work may be reproduced or transmitted in any form or by any means, electronic or mechanical, including photocopying, recording or by any information storage and retrieval system, without the prior written permission of the publisher.

Published by Black Chili Limited

For more information, please email
publications@blackchili.co.uk

Every reasonable care has been taken in the creation of this publication. The publisher and author cannot accept any responsibility for any loss or damage resulting from the use of materials, information and recommendations found in the text of this publication, or from any errors or omissions that may be found in this publication or that may occur at a future date, except as expressly provided in law.

Masculine pronouns such as 'He' and 'His' are used throughout this publication for consistency, but no gender bias is intended.

AWS Certified

Solution Architect Associate
Study Guide & Exam Prep

Introduction

Cloud computing has completely transformed the technology landscape, in what seems like a heartbeat. This guide is designed for readers with a level of familiarity with both IT infrastructure concepts and Amazon Web Services (AWS). It assumes you are preparing for an associate level exam on AWS components, and is not intended to provide an introduction to the fundamentals of AWS.

The contents of this book were built by the author from his journey in passing the related exam.

Cloud Computing is the delivery of computing services such as servers, storage, databases, networking, software, analytics, intelligence, and more, over the Cloud (Internet).

Cloud Computing provides an alternative to the traditional datacentre. If you own or operate a datacentre, everything needs to be managed – the premises, power, cooling, purchasing and installing hardware, virtualisation, installing the operating system, and any applications, setting up the networking, routing and network security, and data storage. You are then responsible for the full lifecycle – all the maintenance and eventual decommissioning.

But if we choose Cloud Computing, a third-party cloud vendor is responsible for datacentre operations. They also provide a wide variety of servers, software, storage and platform as a service options. We consume whatever services we wish and are typically charged based on usage.

There are three main flavours of Cloud Computing – Public, Private, and Hybrid.

Public Cloud services are owned and operated by a third-party cloud service provider. They deliver computing resources such as servers, software, and storage. Providing a virtual datacentre over the internet. Amazon AWS would be an example of a Public Cloud service.

Private Cloud services are those built to be exclusively used inside a single business or organisation. A private cloud may be physically located in company-operated premises or hosted by a third-party. Private Clouds typically consist of server and storage infrastructure, upon which many servers and services are virtualised. This is typically a much more costly option.

Hybrid cloud is a combination of public and private clouds, bridged together by technology that allows data and applications to be shared between them. Hybrid cloud provides flexibility and more deployment options to the business.

Cloud services are typically badged 'as a Service', and you'll see 'aaS' a good deal. Examples of high-level service types are:

Infrastructure as a Service (IaaS): Think of IaaS as the rental of traditional infrastructure elements like servers, storage, networks, operating systems and such from a cloud service vendor. We can create virtual machines running Windows or Linux and install anything we need on them as required. Using IaaS gives the customer freedom from hardware maintenance and hypervisor management, but everything beyond that is managed by the customer. The customer is in total control of systems running on managed infrastructure. AWS EC2 would be an example of IaaS.

Platform as a Service (PaaS): The PaaS family of services provide on-demand environments for developing, testing, delivering, and managing software applications. The customer is responsible for applications and services, and the PaaS vendor provides the ability to deploy and run them. PaaS lacks the total customer control of IaaS, but has the advantage of reducing customer responsibility to the application tier, with everything else managed by the cloud services vendor. RDS would be an example of a PaaS service.

Software as a Service (SaaS): SaaS covers the centrally hosted and managed software services provided direct to end-users. SaaS delivers software over the internet, on-demand, and typically on a subscription basis. Microsoft One Drive, Dropbox, WordPress, Office 365, and Amazon Kindle. SaaS is used to minimize the operational cost to the maximum extent.

In the following pages you will find everything the author collated in his study of Amazon's Certified Solution Architect – Associate. This is an associate level qualification, and a solid familiarity with Amazon AWS is expected. Appreciation of common IT infrastructure concepts is expected.

The AWS Solution Architect Associate examination has no pre-requisites, but if you find the material in this book too advanced, consider completing the AWS Cloud Practitioner material first as an introduction.

About the Author

I left University with an English Literature degree and like most people with English degrees who have no inclination to go into teaching; I had no idea what I was going to do. I fell into a resourcing job for a recruitment company... calling people and talking to them on the phone about technology jobs I didn't understand and getting paid minimum wage. I have that terrible job to thank for setting my future direction.

My last day at that company started uneventfully enough, until one of the many people I called that day unwittingly showed me the light. He was pretty horrible actually – I'd called him regarding a contract that was obviously some way beneath him. He was direct, to put it mildly – and his parting words were, 'So you can update your records, I wouldn't take a permanent role for less than £250K'. **Two hundred and fifty *thousand* pounds?** (and this was in 1999!) At the rate I was going that would be 25 years' wages. And that was my light bulb moment.

I looked at the skills required for some of the serious consultancy roles, I was spending my days trying to fill, then researched what the jobs that fed those sorts of positions were. Having followed my nose to the entry level of the field, I set about acquiring the skills required to get through the door. I worked my way through the ranks in several jobs, which at the time I didn't much appreciate, all of which allowed me to build solid experience with some of the biggest companies in the world.

I studied for professional qualifications on my own time, self-funding courses and exams – investing in myself. I have been Vendor Certified since 1999!

My Certifications include:

- Amazon Certified AWS Solution Architect
- Microsoft Certified Azure Architect Expert
- Microsoft Certified Azure Security Engineer
- Microsoft Certified Azure Administrator
- Microsoft Certified Systems Engineer
- Microsoft Certified Administrator
- Microsoft Certified Professional

As well as many more including TOGAF, ITIL, Forcepoint & ForgeRock.

Certifications have helped me secure ever-more senior positions in large companies and have seen my annual salary increase many times over since I started on the certification trail in 1999. All my cloud certifications have been gained without classroom teaching, using Amazon Whitepapers, and other material freely available on the Internet. Access to, and familiarity with, the AWS Portal and command line tools will be a massive advantage as you approach the exam.

You will find my professional profile on LinkedIn here:

https://www.linkedin.com/in/renhimself/

Global Infrastructure

An overview of the Amazon Web Services high level components and terminology.

AWS Service Areas

Compute, Storage, Databases, Migration and Transfer, Network and Content Delivery, Developer Tools, Robotics, Blockchain, Satellite, Management and Governance, Media Services, Machine Learning, Analytics, Security Identity and Compliance, Mobile. AR & VR, Application Integration, AWS Cost Management, Customer Engagement, Business Applications, Desktop & App streaming, IOT, Game Development.

Regions

A region is geographical as in north America, Europe etc with each having at least 2 availability zones. An availability zone is basically a datacentre (possibly several in close proximity).

GovCloud

AWS for Government entities and their authorized contractors only.

Edge locations

Edge Locations are AWS endpoints used for caching content, typically CloudFront CDN.

Owner

An owner in AWS is the identity and email address associated with the account.

Identity Access Management

IAM allows setup of users, groups, roles and permissions and policies to grant access to the AWS platform.

Centralised control, shared access, granular permissions, identity federation, MFA, PCI DSS Compliant. Policies are constructed with documents in JSON format. In IAM, the changes and settings are global rather than region specific.

Users

Programmatic access enables access key ID and secret access key for AWS API, CLI, SDK and other dev tools. Access keys are generated by default, can be unselected. Users have no permissions when first created.

When a programmatic user is first created the key and secret are supplied, csv can be downloaded. These details will never be shown again so save them. If you fail to, or forget them, a new key and secret can be generated in the security credentials section of the user account. They are also stored in the .AWS folder in user home directory in EC2 instance logged in to, possible security risk with Amazon recommending the use of roles.

Groups

Group creation – AWS have many policies created by job function. You can also create custom policies.

Access key ID and secret only allow programmatic access, not console login.

How can you get notification if charges exceed a threshold? Set up a billing alarm under CloudWatch, which uses SNS topics to email you an alert if a threshold is crossed.

S3 - Simple Storage Service

A safe place to store files, object-based storage spread across multiple devices and facilities. 5TB maximum file size, unlimited storage.

S3 Buckets, basically folders. You are permitted 100 per account by default

Naming

Universal namespace, so bucket names must be globally unique:

- yourname.s3.amazonAWS.com
  (North Virginia), or;
- yourname.region.amazonaws.com

S3 URL: Styles - Virtual style puts your bucket name 1st, s3 2nd, and the region 3rd. Path style puts s3 1st and your bucket as a sub domain. Legacy Global endpoint has no region. S3 static hosting can be your own domain or your bucket name 1st, s3-website 2nd, followed by the region. AWS are in the process of phasing out Path style, and support for Legacy Global Endpoint format is limited and discouraged. However, it is still useful to be able to recognize them should they show up in.

Object Availability & Consistency

When you upload a file, you will get an http 200 code back to confirm successful upload.

Objects consist of - Key (the name), Value (the data), Version ID (for versioning), Metadata (data about data), Sub resources like ACLs and Torrents.

Data consstency in S3. Read after write for new objects — as soon as an object is uploaded, it can be read. Eventual consistency for overwrite and delete which takes some time to propoxate — updates to existing file or deletion take time to propoxate, so you may not get the latest version right away.

99.99% availability, with 99.9% guaranteed. 11 9s guaranteed for durability (unlikely to be lost)

s3 features tiered storage, lifecycle management, versioning, encryption, MFA on deletes, ACLs and bucket policies.

S3 storage classes

Standard has 99.99% availability, 11 9s durability, stored redundantly across multiple devices in multiple facilities and designed to sustain the failure of 2 facilities concurrently.

S3-IA (infrequently accessed, used to be known as RRS reduced redundancy storage) has lower fees, but a retrieval fee — worthwhile for rarely used data.

S3 One Zone — IA, an even lower cost option for infrequently accessed data without the multiple availability zone resilience.

S3 Intelligent Tiering designed to optimise cost by automatically moving data to the most cost-effective tier based on usage. Latency is in the milliseconds for all classes outside of glacier.

S3 Glacier is for data archiving with retrieval times configurable from minutes to hours. Very cost effective. S3 Glacier Deep Archive is the lowest cost storage class with a 12hr retrieval time.

Charging & Transfer

S3 charging — storage volume, number of requests, storage management, data transfer pricing, transfer acceleration, cross region replication.

Cross region replication is the automatic replication of an S3 bucket from one region to another for availability and/or resilience.

S3 transfer acceleration enables fast and easy transfer of files over long distances between users and S3 using CloudFront edge locations and routing over an optimised network path. Basically, users upload to edge, and the objects then use the amazon backbone to get back to S3.

You cannot install an OS or database on object-based storage, so no S3 for them.

READ S3 FAQS! Visit amazonaws.com and familiarize yourself with the S3 questions when preparing for the exam.

S3 buckets can only be deleted if empty. Bucket settings can be cloned from an existing when creating new. Versioning and server access logging can be enabled. Object level logging also possible. Buckets are not publicly accessible by default.

Permissions can be set using ACLs to buckets and the individual objects within them. Controlling access to buckets can be achieved with ACLs or policies.

S3 Exam tips - Buckets are a universal name space. Uploads to S3 return an http 200 success code. Tiers are S3, S3-IA, S3-IA One Zone, S3 Intelligent Tiering, Glacier, Glacier Deep Archive.

S3 Pricing

S3 Pricing Tiers. The cost is made up of storage fees per GB, requests and retrievals, data transfer, management and replication.

Storage fees — S3 standard $0.023/GB first 50TB/month, next 450TB $0.022/GB/month over 500TB $0.021/GB/Month. S3 Intelligent tiering is the same but adds IA at $0.0125/GB/Month, but IA has a $0.0025/month management fee per 1000 objects.

S3 IA is $0.0125/GB/Month, S3 IA One Zone is $0.01/GB/Month. Glacier is $0.004/GB/Month and Glacier Deep Archive is $0.00099/GB/Month.

Understand how to get the best value — Intelligent tiering is often a good answer unless you need Glacier or have a massive number of objects.

S3 security & encryption

Encryption in transit is achieved with TLS/SSL. Encryption at rest is achieved by S3 managed keys (SSE-S3), AWS key managed service, managed keys (SSE-KMS) or server-side encryption with customer provided keys — SSE-C. Client-side encryption also possible prior to S3 upload.

Versioning

S3 versioning. Once versioning has been enabled on a bucket it cannot be disabled, only suspended.

Versioning comes with MFA delete, and integrates with lifecycle rules.

Uploading a new version of the file removes the public setting, so it will need re-enabling for access. Old versions remain public once set.

Versioning can increase storage requirement significantly, depending on rate of change. Policies to remove old versions after a period of time may be wise.

Deletion — with versions hidden the deletion of a file places a delete marker on the file... which is just another version. Delete the version with the delete marker and the file is restored. With versions shown, deleting a file version will result in deletion.

Versioning enables MFA delete for an additional layer of security.

Lifecycle management with S3 — automates the transition of objects between storage tiers, or their expiration. Lifecycle rules can be applied to all objects in a bucket, or all objects with specified tags. Can be enabled for current version, previous versions, or both.

Organisations

AWS Organisations — an account management service that enables consolidation of multiple AWS accounts into an organisation you create and centrally manage.

Best practice is to use root for billing only, do not deploy any resources there. Use OUs off root to compartmentalise management and access. Consolidated billing helps reduce cost by aggregating all resources in to one billing account. One bill per AWS account and volume pricing discounts.

Once you create an organisation you can invite other AWS accounts to your organisation by email or account ID or create new accounts within your organisation.

Policies can be applied to OUs (Service control policy) that restrict members of an OU from accessing services.

Always enable MFA on the root account and use a complex password. Root (paying) account should be used for billing only, no resources deployed to root.

Sharing S3 buckets across accounts

There are 3 ways to share S3 buckets across accounts. Bucket policies and IAM — programmatic access only. Bucket ACLs and IAM, again programmatic access only. Or cross account IAM roles, which will give programmatic and console access.

Role can be created, pasting in the ID for another AWS account in 'accounts that can use this role'. Grant necessary roles to the alternate AWS account. Cannot use the root account of the alternate AWS account, so additional users must exist. Use switch role to access resources permitted in other accounts.

Cross region replication requires versioning to be enabled on the source destination S3 bucket. Replication can be for the whole bucket or on prefix tags. It can be within a region or cross-region. Destination bucket can be created during replication setup, and access roles can be selected or defined during replication rule creation. Changes and additions post-replication setup are replicated, but any objects already in the bucket will need to be manually uploaded. Delete markers and deletions are not replicated.

S3 Transfer acceleration uses CloudFront edge networks to transfer files to S3 over the Amazon backbone. Upload URLs are distinct. Amazon have a tool that will compare direct upload speeds to the transfer acceleration service.

Cloudfront

CloudFront is a CDN, a system of distributed servers that delivers web content to users from a more local point than the originating system, which improves performance. Cached at edge locations, from origin in S3, EC2, load balancer or route 53. A distribution is a collection of edge locations. First user consumes the content by downloading it from source, it is then cached at local edge location for a configured time. Subsequent users will pull the same content from the edge cache, until the cache TTL expires. Caches can be cleared (invalidating the cache), but this is chargeable.

CloudFront is dynamic and will automatically use the best locations for users. Web distribution is used for web content, RTMP is used for media streaming.

Edge locations are not read only, they can also be written to (See S3 Transfer Acceleration).

CloudFront is global, not regional. Can cache a bucket, or a folder within. Access can be restricted to signed URLs or cookies. WAFs can also be used to protect distributions.

CloudFront distributions can take up to an hour to create, and must be disabled before they can be deleted, which can take 15 mins to complete. A specific domain name is provided for CloudFront edge location.

To remove from edge locations, create invalidations. An invalidation can remove specific files or folders, or everything. Invalidating will remove objects from edge locations but incurs a charge.

Snowball

Snowball is a petabyte scale data transfer solution that can securely get data into or out of AWS S3. Gets around network costs, long transfer times and security concerns. Comes in 50TB or 80TB variants. Tamper-resistant enclosures, 256-but encryption and TPM modules to ensure full chain of custody of data. Once transfer is complete, AWS performs software erasure of the snowball appliance.

Snowball edge is a 100TB device that has compute capability. It can be used for data transfer as above but can also be used as local storage for remote or offline locations. Snowball edge devices can also be clustered together for local storage, with no need for cloud access.

Snowmobile is an Exabyte scale data transfer service used to move massive amounts of data to AWS. Up to 100PB per Snowmobile in a 45ft ruggedized shipping container. Secure, fast and cost-effective.

Snowball transfer becomes desirable vs T3 transfer at 2TBps. 100Mbps transfer at 5TB and vs 1Gbps transfer at 60TB.

Storage Gateway

Storage Gateway connects on-prem software appliances with cloud-based storage to bridge on-prem and cloud. Storage gateway can be virtual or physical as a VM, runs on VMWare or Hyper-V. Once the gateway is associated with your AWS account, it can be configured in the management portal.

Gateway Types

2 types – File gateway is NFS & SMB for file storage. Volume gateway is iSCSI for stored and cached volumes, plus tape gateway, which is a virtual tape library.

File gateway enables the storage of objects in S3, accessible via NFS mount points. Once objects are in S3, they can be managed just like any other S3 object.

Volume gateway – stored volumes presents apps with disk volumes using the iSCSI block protocol. Data in these volumes can be backed up as snapshots of the volumes and stored in the cloud as EBS snapshots Snapshots are incremental backups that capture only changed blocks, and snapshot storage is compressed to minimise storage charges. A way to store virtual disks in the cloud. Stored volumes allow for storage of primary data locally, while backing up to AWS. Stored volumes are entire data sets, any changes are written locally and then backed up to S3.

Cache volumes let you use S3 as your primary data storage whilst retaining frequently accessed data locally in the storage gateway. You can create volumes up to 32TB and attach them as iSCSI devices to on-prem systems. The gateway stores data in S3 but retains recently read data in on-prem storage – 1GB to 32TB for cached volumes.

Tape Gateway facilitates the archiving of data to AWS cloud but storing data on virtual tape cartridges. Each tape gateway has a media changer and tape drives to enable client backup apps to connect via iSCSI. Supported by NetBackup, Backup Exec, Veeam and many others.

Athena Vs Macie

Athena vs Macie. Athena is an interactive query service which allows the analysis of data in S3 using standard SQL in a serverless manner. Like turning S3 into a giant SQL DB. Charges are per query and by TB scanned. Athena can be used to query logs, generate business reports, analyse AWS cost and usage reports and run queries on click-stream data. Macie works on PII data and is a security service that uses machine learning and NLP to discover, classify and protect sensitive data in S3. It uses AI to recognise sensitive data, has a dashboard, reports and alerts. It works directly in S3 and can also analyse CloudTrail logs. Very useful for PCI-DSS compliance and for preventing identity theft.

Amazon Athena supports a wide variety of data formats like CSV, TSV, JSON, or Text files and also supports open source columnar formats such as Apache ORC and Apache Parquet.

EC2

EC2 – Elastic Compute Cloud. Allows the rapid scaling of server infrastructure up or down in minutes, reducing timescales and Capex. The EC2 hypervisor is built on Xen and Nitro.

Pricing

Pricing models – On demand, priced by the hour. Good for low cost and no up-front payment, no commitment. Also good for applications with short term, spiky or unpredictable workloads that cannot be interrupted. Good for initial app testing on AWS.

Reserved provides capacity reservation for 1 year or 3 years – the more you pay up front, the more you save. Good for steady state or predictable usage, apps that require reserved capacity, and users able to make upfront payments to reduce overall cost. Different types – standard reserved instances, up to 75% off depending on amount payed upfront. Convertible reserved instances allow types of instance to be changed. Scheduled reserved instances are good for boxing resources to specific timeframes.

Spot instances are where AWS has spare capacity; prices are dropped to encourage use. Instances are taken away when prices go beyond your bid price. Good for apps that have flexible start and end times, apps that need very low cost and users that have an urgent need for large amounts of compute capacity. If the instance is terminated by Amazon, you will not be charged for a partial hour of usage. If you terminate the instance you will be charged for any hour in which the instance ran.

Dedicated hosts are physical EC2 servers dedicated for your use. Useful in environments that may not support multi-tenant virtualisation, licensing that does not support cloud deployments, and can be purchased on demand.

Configuration Options

Instance types. F – FPGA, I – IOPS, G – Graphics, H – High disk throughput, T – Cheap and General purpose, D – Density, R – RAM, M – main choice for general purpose apps, C – Compute, P – Graphics (Pics), X – Extreme Memory, Z – Extreme CPU and memory, A – ARM, U – Bare metal FIGHTDRMCPXZAU. The numbers are the generation, and not important.

When provisioning an EC2 instance, selecting availability zone is somewhat random. '1a' the first time you spin one up may differ to '1a' the next time.

Monitoring by default every 5 minutes, more frequent monitoring requires that detailed monitoring be selected.

Configure security group creates a virtual firewall.

It is now possible to encrypt root storage volumes.

Delete on termination is not selected by default on additional storage volumes. Root volumes are deleted on termination by default.

Termination protection is turned off by default, must be manually selected.

Security Groups

Security groups – any change on a security group takes effect immediately. The rules are stateful, so anything allowed in will also be allowed out. All outbound traffic is allowed by default.

Cannot block ports or source addresses with security groups or create deny rules – have to use NACLs instead. All inbound traffic is blocked by default though. and security groups are used to allow specific services either globally or from specified addresses.

It is possible to add an EC2 instance to more than one security group, and any number of instances can be a member of a security group

Disks

- EBS – elastic block store. A virtual block storage volume in the cloud. Each volume is automatically replicated within its availability zone to protect against component failure. 5 types – General purpose, provisioned IOPS, Throughput optimised HDD, Cold HDD, EBS Magnetic.

- General Purpose (gp2) SSD is designed to balance price and performance. 16K IOPS per volume.

- Provisioned IOPS (io1) SSD is for when IOPS requirement exceeds 16K per volume in the above, 64K IOPS.

- Throughput optimised (st1) is for big data and data warehousing, frequent access and throughput intense 500 IOPS.

- Cold HDD (sc1) is for file servers and is a low-cost HDD option for less frequent access 260 IOPS.

- EBS Magnetic (standard) is a previous generation offering, but still available and for use cases where data is infrequently accessed 40-200 IOPS.

EBS volumes will always be in the same availability zone as their related EC2 instance

EBS Volumes can be made larger on the fly but can take time to take effect. OS changes may be required – a re-partitioning of the drive for all space to be usable.

The root volume can have type changed to provisioned IOPS or magnetic, and can be increased in size, but not decreased – all on the fly.

To move an EC2 instance or EBS volume to a different availability zone, take a snapshot, create an image from the snapshot using hardware assisted virtualisation. Launch the AMI (Amazon Machine Image) and change the subnet for a different availability zone. The AMI can also be copied to a different region. That image can then be used to deploy EC2 instances to new regions.

When an AMI is copied then launched the launch permissions, tags and bucker permissions are not inherited from the image. They must be manually applied.

Snapshots exist in S3 – point in time copies of volumes. If taking a snapshot of an EBS rot volume, it is best practice to stop the related EC2 instance before taking the snapshot, but you can take the snapshot whilst it is running.

Volumes must be detached before they can be deleted.

By default, when an EC2 instance is terminated the root volume will be deleted but additional volumes will not.

EBS vs Instance Store. AMIs can be selected based on region, OS, 64x or 32x, launch permissions or storage of root device – instance store (ephemeral storage) or EBS backed volume. For EBS volumes, the root device is launched from and EBS volume created from an EBS snapshot. For instance, store the root device is launched from an AMI instance store volume from a template in S3.

If you build an EC2 instance from an instance store AMI and want to add additional instance store volumes, it can only be done during initial setup. On the instance is created only EBS volumes can be added.

Instance store backed instances can only be rebooted or terminated, they cannot be stopped. This also means you cannot stop and start to move hypervisor in the event of issues. Hypervisor failure means the loss of the system and all data.

Network

ENI vs ENA vs EFA. ENI – elastic network interface, a virtual NIC. EN is enhanced networking (ENA is a subtype) – uses single root I/O virtualisation to provide high performance networking. EFA is Elastic Fabric Adapter, which is a network device you can attach to an EC2 instance to accelerate high performance computing (HPC) and machine learning applications.

Use ENI for additional non-production networks, for using network and security appliances in your VPC, for creating dual homed instances, or to create a low budget, high availability solution.

Enhanced networking is a method of device virtualisation for higher I/O performance and lower CPU compared to traditional network interfaces. Provides higher bandwidth and lower latency. No additional charge, though EC2 instance does have to support it.

ENA supports network speeds of up to 100Gbps, older instances may use Intel 82599 Virtual Function (VF) which is limited to 10Gbps. Chose ENA over VF.

HPC applications and machine learning, always choose elastic fabric adapter. These bypass the OS (Linux only) for lower latency and improved performance.

Encryption

Encrypted Root Device Volumes & Snapshots. Root volumes can now be encrypted on creation. To encrypt an unencrypted root volume, take a snapshot, copy the snapshot but choose to encrypt the copy, create an image from the encrypted snapshot hen use the image to launch a new EC2 instance. You cannot take an encrypted image and build it on a non-encrypted volume.

Volumes restored from encrypted snapshots are encrypted automatically, as are snapshots of encrypted volumes. Snapshots can be shared with other AWS accounts, or made public, but only if unencrypted.

Monitoring

CloudWatch is a monitoring service for AWS resources and apps running on AWS. It can monitor compute, autoscaling groups, elastic load balancers, Route53 health checks, storage and CDN, EBS volumes, storage gateways and CloudFront.

CloudWatch and EC2 – host level metrics can be monitored such as CPU, network, Disk, Status Check. CloudWatch will monitor EC2 every 5 minutes by default. Detailed logging can bring this down to 1 minute.

CloudWatch can use alarms to trigger notifications.

CloudTrail increases visibility of user and resource activity by recording AWS management console actions and API calls. Use CloudTrail to identify users and accounts called AWS, source IPs and time/date.

CloudWatch is all about performance, CloudTrail is all about auditing.

Detailed monitoring can be enabled during instance creation, or afterwards via the Action menu. Standard metrics are CPU, disk and network. Anything beyond standard display requires custom metric configuration.

Notification alarms can be set for specific metrics, RAM and CPU utilisation for example... emails sent when a specific threshold is reached for a defined period.

Dashboards can be created for monitoring metrics, either regionally or globally.

Logs can be sent to, aggregated and stored in CloudWatch. Events can be set up to give near real-time views of state changes.

AWS Command Line (CLI) is global, and programmatic access is required for a user account to execute command line.

Command line commands are not in the exam, but basic commands are useful, so a review is recommended.

IAM Roles

IAM Roles. Assign a role from EC2 actions menu, create a role with necessary permissions which will then permit use of the command line without the storage of credentials in the user home drive .AWS directory.

Roles are easier to manage than access keys on multiple systems, as well as more secure. They can be assigned to an EC2 instance after creation and they are universal. They can be used in any region.

Metadata

Bootstrap scripts can be used to pipe in command line bash scripts during start-up. Can be very powerful.

EC2 Instance Metadata – used to get information about an instance – curl http://169.254.169.254/latest/meta-data. Can also get bootstrap information from /user-data.

Filesystems

EFS – Elastic File system. A service for EC2 that creates a shareable volume that will automatically grow and shrink as data is added and removed, only pay for what you remove. EFS can be accessed by more than one EC2 instance.

On creation, an EFS volume is added to the default security group and default VPC. Stored across multiple availability zones within a region with read after write consistency.

EFS supports the NFS 4 protocol, and can support thousands of concurrent connections

FSx provides a fully managed native MS Windows file system to enable the move of windows-based apps to AWS. It is built on Windows server. So essentially a Windows File Server. SMB based and supports AD users, ACLS, groups and security policies, as well as DFS namespaces and replication. Choose FSx for Windows system access and SMB.

EFS is a managed NAS file system for EC2 based on NFS, one of the first network file sharing protocols native to Unix and Linux. Choose EFS for Linux shared storage.

Amazon FSx for Lustre is as standard FSx but optimised for compute intensive workloads – high performance computing, Machine Learning, Media processing and electronic design automation. Can process massive datasets with hundreds of GBps throughput, millions of IOPS and sub-millisecond latency. FSx for Lustre can store direct in S3.

Placement Groups

EC2 placement groups. Three types – clustered placement groups, spread placement groups and partitioned placement groups

Clustered placement groups are groups of instances within a single availability zone, ideal for apps that need low latency, high throughput, or both by keeping instances close together. Only certain instances can be launched into clustered placement groups.

Spread placement groups are groups of instances all placed on distinct hardware with separate networking and power in separate racks. Better for resilience. Can also be across multiple availability zones within a region. Use for individual critical EC2 instances. Has a limitation of a maximum of 7 instances per availability zone.

Partition placement groups are similar to the above, but you can have multiple EC2 instances in each partition within a placement group. Each partition is a separate rack with its own power and networking, so any hardware failure impact is limited to a partition. Good for multiple instances in each location – HDFS, HBase and Cassandra. Can also be across multiple availability zones within a region.

Names for placement groups must be unique within your AWS account.

Only compute optimized, GPU, Memory optimised, and storage optimised instances can be put in placement groups. AWS recommend the same EC2 instance types for use in clustered placement groups.

Placement groups cannot be merged.

An existing EC2 instance can be moved to a placement group provided it is in a stopped state. This can be done from the CLI or SDK, but not from the console currently.

Web Application Firewall

Amazon WAF – a Web Application Firewall that lets you monitor HTTP and HTTPS requests that are forwarded to CloudFront, an Application load balancer or API gateway. AWS WAF also lets you control access to your content. An application layer 7 firewall.

Firewall config including source IPs, which query string parameters are allowed to pass to the receiving service. The load balancer, API gateway or CloudFront will then allow or 403 the traffic.

WAF has 3 basic behaviour types – allow everything except things you block, block all except those you allow, or count the requests made that match properties specified.

Protections can be configured based on elements of web requests such as the IP or country a request comes from, values in request headers, strings in requests either specific or regex, the length of requests, the presence of SQL code likely to be malicious or a script likely to be malicious.

If you want to block malicious IPs – use a WAF or network ACLs. To block SQL, scripts etc... use WAF.

Databases

Database Types

RDS – Relational Database Services. A relational database is a bit like giant spreadsheet with tables, rows and fields. Relational databases on AWS can be MSSQL, Oracle, MySQL. PostgreSQL, Amazon Aurora or MariaDB.

2 Key Features – Multi Availability Zones, for resilience and disaster recovery, and read replicas for performance. Multi AZ, in the event of failure AWS will detect and update DNS, redirecting a traffic to an alternate location for the database. In Read replica, all writes are replicated to the replica. IN the event of failure there is no automatic recovery, EC2 instances would need to be updated to reference the new location. The read replica option is useful to spread read load across the replicas. Configure EC2 instances to connect across the replicas – up to 5 copies of a DB.

RDS Provisioned IOPS storage with SQL server – 16TB RDS volume limit.

You can force failover to another availability zone for RDS with a reboot with failover.

Non-relational DBs. Collections = tables, document = row, key value pairs = fields/columns.

Data warehousing is used for business intelligence. tools like Cognos, Jaspersoft, SQL server reporting services, Oracle Hyperion, SAP NetWeaver. Used to pull in large and complex datasets.

Online Transaction Processing differs from online analytics processing differs in terms of the queries types run. OLTP will pull up an order number ad display all values relevant to it. OLAP can pull in a huge number of records, example – profit in a specific region for a specific product range. All orders would need to be queried for location and product, values collated and interpreted.

Data Warehousing databases use a different type of architecture both from a DB and infrastructure perspective.

DynamoDB is Amazon's No SQL solution. DynamoDB can support Binary objects up to 400kb. DynamoDB is automatically replicates across AZs.

RedShift is Amazon's data warehousing solution for OLAP.

ElastiCache is a service to deploy, operate and scale an in-memory cache in the cloud. The service improves performance of web applications by allowing retrieval of information from memory caches instead of relying on disks. ElastiCache can take a huge load off the database for frequent identical queries.

ElastiCache supports two open-source in-memory caching engines – Memcached and Redis.

RDS

RDS Database create does not give a DB a name by default, meaning you have to use admin tools to connect to add one. Easier just to do it in setup via advanced options.

RDS runs on virtual machines, but you do not have access to them for patching or anything else. RDS is not serverless, though there is serverless Aurora.

If you want your application to check RDS for an error, have it look for an error node in the response from the Amazon RDS API.

RDS Backups, Multi AZ and Read Replicas.

2 different types of RDS backups. Automated backups and snapshots. Automated backups allow you to recover your DB to any point in time within the retention period of 35 days. An automated backup is a full daily snapshot , plus transaction logs throughout the day. By restoring the most recent daily backup plus transaction logs it is possible to restore to any point down to a second within the retention period. Automated backups are on by default and stored in S3. Storage is free up to the size of your DB. Backups are taken within a window, and during the backup storage I/O may be suspended. Latency may also be elevated.

Snapshots are point in time and manual. They are stored even after the RDS instance is deleted, unlike automated backups. When you select to delete an RDS instance, you will be asked if you want to take a final snapshot.

Whenever you restore a database from automated backup or snapshot, the restored version will be a new RDS instance with a new DNS endpoint.

Encryption

Encryption at rest is available for MySQL, Oracle, SQL server, PostgreSQL, MariaDB and Aurora using the AWS key management service. Once the RDS instance is encrypted, the data stored in underlying storage is encrypted as are automated backups, read replicas and snapshots.

Resilience

Multi AZ allows you to haven exact copy of your production DB in another AZ. All changes are simultaneously replicated to the standby DB in another AZ. In the event of primary failure, RDS will automatically failover to the standby without admin intervention.

Multi-AZ is for resiliency and DR only, not performance. Available for SQL, Oracle, MySQL, PostgreSQL, MariaDB. Aurora has its own fault tolerance by design. Multi-AZ may make your DB slower and do it in a scheduled maintenance window.

A Read replica is one or more copies of a production DB, which are kept in sync with the production DB. You can have read replicas of read replicas (watch for latency), and a read replica can be promoted to a standalone DB, though that breaks replication. Read replicas allow you to keep read only copies of production DBs to improve the performance of read-heavy workloads by distributing connections to them. Available for Oracle, MySQL, PostgreSQL, MariaDB. Aurora.

Read replicas are for scaling, not DR. Automatic backups are required to deploy a read replica. You can have up to 5 read replica copies of any DB.

Each read replica will have its own DNS end point. You can have read replicas with multi-AZ and can have read replicas in a second region.

Easy way to migrate to Aurora – just take a read replica to Aurora from the action's menu

You can force Multi-AZ failover by rebooting with failover.

Read replica has a master and a replica. The replica can be promoted to a primary.

DynamoDB

DynamoDB is a fast and flexible NoSQL solution for applications that need consistent and single-digit latency at any scale. Fully managed and supports both document and key-value data models. The flexible data model makes it a great fit for mobile, web, gaming, ad-tech, IoT and many others.

DynamoDB is stored on SSD, spread across 3 geographically distinct data centres. 2 modes of operation – eventually consistent reads as default, or strongly consistent reads. Eventual consistent reads see consistency across all copies of data usually within a second. Repeating a read after a short time should return the updated data (best read performance). Strongly consistent reads return results that reflect all writes that received a successful response prior to the read. if your app is OK with 1 second lag with update, eventual is sufficient.

RedShift

RedShift is Amazon's fast and powerful data warehousing service in the cloud. Start from as little as $0.25 per hour with no upfront cost or commitment, and scale to a petabyte or more for $1,000 per terabyte per year. Much cheaper than most other solutions. OLAP – Online Analytics processing – multiple queries against different datasets, plus calculations.

RedShift can be configured as a single node up to 160GB, or multi-node. Multi-node has a leader node to manage client connections and receive queries, and the compute nodes store data and perform the queries and computations. You can have up to 128 compute nodes.

Redshift uses Columnar compression, making it more efficient and able to compress more owing to the sequential nature of the storage. Redshift does not require indexes or materialised views so uses less space. Redshift will automatically select the most appropriate compression scheme based on samples of data.

Massively Parallel Processing (MPP). Redshift automatically distributes data and query load across all nodes. Redshift makes it easy to add nodes to your data warehouse and enables you to maintain fast query performance as data grows.

Redshift backups are enabled by default with a 1-day retention. Backups can be retained up to 35 days. Redshift will always attempt to maintain at least 3 copies of your data, the original and a replica on the compute nodes and a backup in S3. Redshift can also replicate backups in S3 to another region for DR.

Redshift is priced on compute node hours – 1 unit per node per hour. Not charged for leader node. Also charged for backups and data transfer within a VPC.

Comms with Redshift are always SSL, and data at rest is always AES-256. By default, it manages the keys, though HSMs or the key management service can also be used.

Redshift is only available in one AZ, but it can be restored to another in the event of failure.

Amazon Aurora

Aurora is a MySQL and PostgreSQL compatible relational database engine that combines the speed and availability of high-end commercial databases with the simplicity and cost-effectiveness of open source databases.

Up to 5x better performance than MySQL, 3x better than PostgreSQL at a much lower price with similar availability.

Aurora starts with 10GB and scales in 10GB increments to 64TB with storage autoscaling. Compute can scale to 32 vCPUs and 244GB of memory. Two copies of your data are contained in each availability zone with a minimum of 3 availability zones. 6 copies of the data.

Aurora is designed to handle 2 data copy failures without impact to write, and up to three with no impact to read. Aurora storage is also self-healing, data blocks and disks are continuously scanned for errors and repaired automatically.

3 types of Aurora replica. Aurora replicas, you can have 15, MySQL replicas, of which you can have 5, and PostgreSQL which is currently limited to 1. These are read replicas. Aurora replicas are more performant in all respects, Aurora can only have replicas within a region, where MySQL replicas can be in different regions. Aurora is also guaranteed against data loss in failover. Automated failover is only available with Aurora replicas.

Automated backups always enabled on Aurora; you can also take snapshot – both without impact on performance. Snapshots can be shared with other accounts.

Aurora Serverless is an on-demand autoscaling configuration for the MySQL compatible and PostgreSQL compatible editions of Aurora. An Aurora serverless DB cluster automatically starts up, shuts down and scales capacity as required based on application needs. Fantastic for infrequent, intermittent, or unpredictable workloads. Cost is only incurred when the instance is active so if you need high performance at a low cost, look at Aurora serverless.

You can create an Aurora read replica from an RDS database, then promote the replica to complete the migration to Aurora. You can also take a snapshot of a database and restore it to Aurora.

ElastiCache

ElastiCache is a web service that makes it easy to deploy, operate and scale an in-memory cache in the cloud. The service improves the performance of web applications by allowing retrieval of information from fast in-memory caches, instead of relying entirely on slower disk-based databases. Available backed my Memcached or Redis.

Memcached

Memcached is simple and scales horizontally for improved performance. Redis offers advanced data types, rank and sort, publishing and subscribing, multiple AZs, persistence and backup/restore options.

Route 53 DNS

Elastic Load Balancers do not have pre-defined IPv4 addresses, you resolve to them using DNS names.

Alias records can be used for root domains (AKA apex or naked domains), CNAMEs cannot. Given the choice in the exam, always pick an Alias record.

You can buy and register domains in route53, but they can take 3 days to register. You can then create records in the namespace as required.

Routing Policies

Routing policies – simple routing, weighted routing, latency-based routing, failover routing, geolocation routing, geoproxmity routing (traffic flow only), multi value answer routing.

Simple routing policy is 1 record with multiple IP addresses. In the event of a query, all options are returned to a user in a random order – so like DNS round robin... ish. Simply create a record and add multiple addresses against it on separate lines. Cannot use health checks.

Weighted routing policies allow traffic to be split according to assigned weighting percentages, with route53 managing the distribution of the traffic. Create multiple separate records for a particular hostname and assign each a traffic percentage weight and set ID (label). You can also create health checks to monitor the availability of the records and choose whether the records are subject to health checks. If a record fails a health check, it will be removed from Route53 until it passes. You can also set up notifications from health checks.

Latency based routing – enables routing based on lowest latency for each user to give them the fastest response. You create a record in each region where your resource exists, when Route53 receives a query, it selects the latency resource record set for the region with the lowest latency for that user and passes it back to the user.

Failover routing policies – used to create an active/passive setup. Route 53 will monitor the primary site with a health check, and failover to the secondary if the primary becomes unresponsive to health check. The secondary does not have to be associated with a health check, since it is the failover option. Only works for 2 records in a pair.

Geolocation routing policies – geolocation routing allows you to choose where traffic will be sent based on the location of the user. Latency based routing gives performant results, but geolocation assures the destination host for users in a specific location. Location can be expressed in continent or country.

Geoproximity routing (traffic flow only) – routes based on the location of your users and resources. You can choose to route more or less traffic to a location by specifying a bias value. The bias expands or shrinks based on the size of the location the user traffic came from. To use geoproximity routing, you must use Route 53 traffic flow.

Multi value answer policies – the same as simple routing, but you can add health checks to each record set. Only healthy records get returned to queries.

Elastic load balancers do not have IP addresses, so always use CNAMES to reference them.

There is a limit of 50 domains, but that limit can be increased by contacting support.

VPCs

Virtual Private Cloud lets you provision a logically isolated section of the AWS cloud where you can launch resources in a virtual network you define. You have complete control over the environment, including selection of IP address range (1 subnet = 1 availability zone. You cannot have a subnet across availability zones, but you can have multiple subnets within an availability zone), creation of subnets, configuration of routing tables and gateways or IGWs. Network config is easy to customise.

You can create a hardware VPN between your corporate data centre and AWS, to use the AWS cloud as an extension of your DC.

Use network ACLs as a first line of defence, as they allow specific blocking and are stateless. Security groups are next, and stateful.

A bastion server is an EC2 instance in a public subnet, used to connect to an instance in a private subnet.

What do VPCs let you do? Launch instances into a subnet of our choosing, selecting custom IP addresses. Configure routing tables between subnets, create Internet gateways and attach to VPC. Better security control over AWS resources, instance security groups, subnet network ACLs

Default VPC is very easy and allows immediate deployment of instances. All subnets in a default VPC are Internet accessible. Each EC2 instance has a public and private IP.

By default, you can have 5 VPCs in each AWS region

VPC Peering allows connection of 2 VPCs using private IPs. You can peer with other accounts, as well as within your own. There is no transitive peering, one VPC is connected to others – so A connects to B and C, but if A connects to B which connects to C, A will not have access to C. Peering has to be direct point to point. Also possible to peer between regions.

When a new VPC is created, no subnets are created automatically, no Internet Gateway, but there is a routing table, a default network ACL and security group.

A subnet cannot span more than one availability zone.

Auto assign public IP address by default is off on subnet creation.

5 addresses are reserved in a subnet by WAS – .0 for the network, .1 for the router, .2 for the DNS server, .3 for future use and .253 for broadcast.

Only 1 Internet Gateway per VPC.

All new subnets not assigned to a specific route are added to the main route by default. It is therefore best practice to make the main route private and non-internet connected so as to avoid making everything publicly accessible by default.

Security groups do not span VPCs

AZs are randomised across accounts, so US-East-1a might be different on your account to somebody else's.

NAT instances vs NAT gateways

A NAT instance is an EC2 system, which therefore needs to be patched and managed. A NAT gateway is a highly available gateway to allow systems communicate with the internet without becoming public.

NAT Instance – remember to disable source/destination checks on your EC2 instance. A NAT instance must be able to send and receive traffic when the source or destination is not itself. A NAT instance must be in a public subnet, there must be a route out of the public subnet. NAT instances are a bottleneck (can increase instance size) and single point of failure. High availability zones can be created using autoscaling groups, multiple subnets in different AZs and a script to automate failover. NAT instances are always behind a security group.

NAT gateways are redundant inside an Availability zone, but you can only have one gateway in an AZ< and cannot span AZs. They have a throughput of 5Gbps, scaling automatically to 45Gbps. No need to patch OS, and NAT gateways are not associated with security groups. NAT gateways are auto assigned a public IP, just update the routing table for 0.0.0.0/0 to use the NAT gateway for Internet connectivity.

If you only have a NAT gateway in one AZ, and that AZ fails, you risk losing Internet connectivity. Consider a NAT gateway per AZ, and configure routing to use the local AZ.

Network access control lists vs security groups

Network ACLs are associated with VPCs and can only be associated with a single VPC. On creation of a new network ACL, everything in and out is denied.

A VPC comes with a default NACL which allows everything in and out. Custom NACLs can be created, which by default block everything in and out.

A subnet can only be associated with on NACL. Associating a subnet with a NACL breaks association with previous NCAL.

Rule numbers are recommended to increment by 100 each time.

With NACLs being stateless, outbound rules need to be manually created to match inbound

Ephemeral ports – 1024-65535. Short-lived ports for transactions between servers. receiving service normally static. This is done to permit return traffic and are only valid for the duration of communication.

A NAT gateway uses ephemeral ports 1024-65535. Network ACLs are processed in order, so deny rules must be listed before Allow.

Subnets on creation will be associated with the default VPC NACL if no other assignment is provided but can be associated with another you create. They can only be associated with one NACL at any one time.

NACLs are evaluated before security groups.

Block source IPs with NACLs, not security groups. NACLs can deny or allow and are stateless.

Custom VPCs and Elastic Load Balancers – a load balancer needs at least 2 public subnets with internet gateways.

Logging

VPC Flow logs – capture information going to and from network interfaces in your VPC. Flow log data is stored using CloudWatch logs, so after creation the logs can be consumed via CloudWatch, can also be stored in S3.

Flow logs at 3 levels – VPC, Subnet or network interface.

You cannot enable flow logs for VPCs that are peered with your VPC, unless both are in the same AWS account. Flow logs can be tagged.

After a flow log is created, its configuration cannot be changed. Cannot change IAM Role.

DNS traffic is not logged, unless an external DNS server is used. Traffic generated by Windows for amazon windows license activation is also not monitored. Traffic from 189.254.169.254 for metadata is not monitored, nor is DHCP or traffic to the reserved IP of the default VPC router.

Bastion Hosts are servers that are designed to withstand attack. Usually available on the Internet and used for remote access to systems on the private network. A NAT gateway is used to provide internet traffic to EC2 instances in private subnets. You cannot use a NAT gateway as a Bastion Host.

Connectivity

Direct Connect – makes it easy to establish a connection from your premises to AWS, reducing cost, increasing bandwidth and providing a more consistent experience. Useful for high throughput and security. Customer connects to a router owned by them in a Direct Connection (DX location) – AWS partner router also possible, that connects from one cage to an AWS dedicated cage router over cross connect, which connects to AWS over the backbone. Never traverses the Internet.

Steps to set up a VPN over direct connect – create a virtual interface in the direct connect console. This is public virtual. Go to the VPC console VPN connections and create a customer gateway. Create a virtual private gateway. Attach the virtual private gateway to the desired VPC. Select VPN connections and create a new VPN connection. Select the virtual private gateway and the customer gateway. Once VPN is available, set up the VPN on the customer gateway or firewall.

Global Accelerator

Global Accelerator – create accelerators to improve availability and performance of applications used by a global audience. By default, global accelerator provides you with two public IP addresses that you associate with the accelerator. You can also bring your own.

User connects to edge location, which connects to the AWS global accelerators. They then decide which endpoint group to send the traffic to based on proximity, endpoint health and weighting. Onward to endpoint groups, and finally endpoints.

Global accelerator includes the following components – Static IP addresses, Accelerator, DNS name, Network Zone, Listener, Endpoint Group, Endpoint.

On creation, global accelerator assigns each accelerator a DNS name that points to the static IPs assigned. You can route to it by name or IP or create your own DNS records to point to the accelerator.

A global accelerator network zone is like an AZ for global accelerator. It services the static IPs for your accelerator from a unique subnet. It is an isolated unit with its own physical infrastructure. If one of the two addresses becomes unavailable, clients can retry on the other.

A listener processes inbound connections from clients to global accelerator based on port or port range and protocol. Supports both TCP and UDP. Each listener has one or more endpoint groups, and traffic is forwarded to endpoints in one of the groups. You associate endpoint groups with listeners by specifying the regions that you want to distribute traffic to. Traffic is distributed to optimal endpoints.

Each endpoint group is associated with a region, and each group includes one or more endpoints in a region. You can adjust the of traffic by using the traffic dial setting. The traffic dial enables easy performance testing for new releases across regions.

Endpoints can be network load balancers, application load balancers, EC2 instances, or Elastic IP addresses. An application load balancer endpoint can be internet facing or internal. Traffic is routed to endpoints based on config such as endpoint weight to specify the proportion of traffic routed to each. Weight can be up to 255.

You can configure an accelerator to always direct a source IP to a specific endpoint to maintain affinity.

Accelerators must be disabled before deletion.

VPC Endpoints enable you to connect your VPC to supported AWS services and VPN endpoint services powered by private link, without an internet gateway, NAT device, VPN connection or AWS direct connection. Instances in your VPC do not require public IPs to communicate with resources if the service, as traffic between your VPC and the service does not leave the Amazon network.

Endpoints

Endpoints are virtual devices, horizontally scaled, redundant and highly available.

2 types of VPC endpoint – interfaces and gateways. An interface endpoint is an elastic network interface with a private IP that serves as an entry point for AWS supported services. Gateway endpoints are supported by S3 and Dynamo DB.

High Availability

AWS Load Balancer types – Application, Network and Classic.

Load Balancer Types

Application Load Balancers are layer 7 and application aware, used primarily for HTTP/HTTPS and are more intelligent than classic load balancers.

Network load balancers are used for TCP load balancing where extreme network performance is required, operating at the layer 4 connection layer. They can handle millions of requests per second at very low latency. Also provide static IPs.

A Classic load balancer is a legacy elastic load balancer. You can load balance HTTP/HTTPS and use layer 7 features like x-forwarding and sticky sessions, but classic load balancers are not application aware. You can use strict layer 4 load balancing for apps that purely rely on TCP. If an app stops responding, a classic load balancer will respond with a 504 error.

A 504 means a problem with the application, not the load balancer.

Configuration

Logged IPs come from the load balancer. To find the originating client IP look for the X-Forwarded-For header in logs.

An internal load balancer is configured within a private subnet. Advanced config lets you choose which subnet to deploy in to.

No IP given for a Classic or Application Load Balancer, always addressed via DNS.

Instances monitored by ELB are always either InService or OutofService.

Sticky sessions allow you to bind a user session to a specific EC2 instance, instead of the classic load balancer behaviour of routing each request to the instance with the smallest load. Sticky sessions can also be enabled for application load balancers, but traffic will be sent to the target group level.

Cross Zone Load Balancing enables load balancers to distribute traffic to destinations across AZs, resulting in an event distribution across the end points. Without it, traffic would only be split at the AZ level, which depending on the number of endpoints in each AZ could result in an uneven distribution beyond AZ level.

Path patterns. You can create a listener with rules to forward requests based on the URL path. This is known as path-based routing. You can run general requests to one target group and requests to render images to another, for example.

Autoscaling

Autoscaling has 3 components – Groups, Configuration Templates and Scaling Options.

Groups are logical collections of services – app servers, webservers or DB servers for example.

Groups use a configuration template to specify AMI ID, instance type, key pair, security group and block device mapping – basically all the elements required to start up an EC2 instance.

The conditions on which a group scales, either based on the occurrence of specific conditions or to a schedule. 5 scaling options – maintain current instance levels at all times (if an unhealthy instance is found it will be replaced),

Scale manually (all you specify is the number of instances, auto scaling makes the necessary changes to instances), scale based on schedule (scaling actions performed automatically on a schedule you set. Useful to respond to a predictable pattern), scale on demand (most popular – scales in response to demand thresholds being met – CPU or RAM utilisation for example), use predictive scaling. Predictive scaling uses previous performance indicators to predict when scaling is required and respond accordingly. Use EC2 scaling and AWS scaling combine to scale resources across multiple services to maintain optimal availability and performance.

Auto scaling will distribute instances across availability zones in the same manner as the instances being replaced.

If you delete an autoscaling group, the instances created by it are also automatically deleted (terminated).

HA Architecture – always plan for failure.

Auto-Build

CloudFormation – automatically scripted build infrastructure stacks, with sample templates available. Quick start gives access to some very complicate deployments.

Rollback – specify alarms for CloudFront to monitor. Changes will be rolled back by CloudFormation if these alarm thresholds are crossed.

AWS Elastic Beanstalk – designed for developers to easily deploy basic services with a single click and no AWS knowledge. It can also be scaled easily. You upload your code; AWS analyses it and figures out what it needs to deploy. Elastic Beanstalk will handle the details of capacity provisioning, load balancing, scaling and application health monitoring.

Applications

Amazon's seemingly endless (and ever-growing) list of applications and services are not all featured in the Solution Architect Associate exam. Those that do appear in the exam can be found in this section. Review the AWS Console and Whitepapers to understand what the rest of the applications are for, but it is unlikely greater depth than that will be useful in an exam situation.

Simple Queue Service (SQS)

A message queue that can be used to store messages while waiting for a computer to process them. A distributed queue system that enables web service applications to quickly and reliably queue messages that one component in the application generates to be consumed by another. It is a temporary repository for messages that await processing.

Using SQS you can decuple application components to run independently, and any component can store messages in failsafe queues. Messages can contain up to 256KB of text in any format, and any component can retrieve them programmatically using the SQS API. The messages can go beyond the 256KB but are then stored in S3.

2 queue types. Standard queues and FIFO queues. Standard is default, almost unlimited message per second and guarantee delivery

at least once. More than one message may be delivered, and they may be delivered out of order, though they provide best effort ordering... not a guarantee. If an app cannot cope with multiple copies of a message or messages out of sequence, use FIFO.

FIFO assures messages will be delivered in order, message preserved until a consumer processes and deletes it. No duplicates. FIFO also supports message groups that allow multiple ordered message groups in a single queue. FIFO is limited to 300 transactions per second but have all the capabilities of standard queues.

SQS is pull, not push. Need an ECS instance polling the queue.

Messages are kept in the queue between 1 minute and 14 days. The default is 4 days.

Visibility timeout – the amount of time a message is invisible in the queue after a reader picks it up. Provided the job is processed before the timeout expires the message is deleted. If not, it becomes visible again, which is what can result in the same message being delivered twice. The visibility timeout can be increased up to 12 hours to overcome this.

SQS regular short polling returns immediately, long polling doesn't return a response until a message arrives in the queue, or the long poll times out. You can reduce EC2 poll cost by using long polling. Long polling is configured in seconds.

Anywhere you see 'decoupling' think SQS.

Simple Workflow Service (SWF)

Simple Workflow Service (SWF) is a web service used to coordinate work across different components. It enables a wide range of use-cases including media processing, web application backends, business process workflows and analytics pipelines to be designed as a coordination of tasks. Tasks represent the invocation of processing steps by code, web calls, human interaction and scripts. SWF is a way to combine the digital with manual tasks. Used in the Amazon warehouse to deal with picking and packing an incoming web order. SWF Workflows can last up to 1 year.

SWF is task oriented, SQS is message oriented. SWF ensures a task is only assigned once, SQS you have to deal with possible multiple messages (FIFO). SWF keeps track of events in an application, where in SQS you have to implement your own app-level tracking, especially if you're using multiple queues.

SWF actor – workflow starter that initiate a process (a website for instance), and deciders that control the flow of the execution. In the event of failure, deciders decide what to do next. Activity workers carry out the activity tasks.

Actors = SWF, Messages = SQS.

Simple Notification Service (SNS)

SNS – Simple Notification Service. Makes it easy to set up, operate and send notifications from the cloud. Easy and cost effective to send messages from an application to users, or other apps.

You can do push notifications to apple/google/windows/android and to china via baidu cloud push.

Can also deliver SMS texts, or email via SQS, or to any HTTP endpoint.

Can group multiple endpoints using topics. A topic is an access point for allowing recipients to subscribe to copies of notifications. A topic can support multiple client types, and SNS will format the messages appropriately for each type.

All messages stored across availability zones.

SNS benefits – push based (no polling), simple APIs, flexible message delivery, inexpensive pay as you go, web based console and point and click interface.

Elastic Transcoder

A media transcoder in the cloud to convert from original source to other formats. Presets for popular output formats. Pay based on minutes transcoding and the resolution transcoded at.

API Gateway

API Gateway – a fully managed service that makes it easy for Devs to publish, maintain, monitor and secure APIs at any scale.

Users connect to API gateway, who are then redirected to Lambda, EC2, DynamoDB or whatever AWS service is appropriate to the API and application.

API Gateway can expose HTTPS endpoints to define a RESTful API, serverlessly connect to services like Lambda and DynamoDB. It can also send each API endpoint to a different target. Runs at very low cost and scales automatically.

Usage can be tracked and controlled with API keys. Requests can be throttled to prevent attack and can be CloudWatch connected for monitoring. Also enables maintenance of multiple API versions.

Define an API. Define resources and nested resources (http paths), then set http methods (get, put etc), set security and choose targets in EC2 or Lambda etc. Set request and response transformations.

Deployed to a stage, using API gateway domain by default although custom domains can be used. It now supports AWS certificate manager for free SSL certs.

API caching is a way to cache an endpoint response to reduce the number of calls made, as well as latency. When caching is enabled for a stage, API gateway caches responses for a specified TTL in seconds.

Same-origin policy – a browser allows a script in a webpage to access data in a second webpage, but only if both have the same origin to prevent cross-site scripting attacks (xss). Some tools, like Curl and Postman, ignore the convention.

Cross-Origin Resource Sharing (CORS)

CORS can be used to overcome the same-origin policy from a server point of view. It is CORS that enables data to be served from an EC2 instance that may exist in S3, for example. Browser makes an http options call; the server responds with a list of domains approved for the action. An error 'origin policy cannot be read at the remote resource?' means CORS needs to be enabled on the API gateway.

Kinesis

Kinesis is used for streaming data is data that is generated continuously by thousands of data sources, typically sent simultaneously and small in size. Kinesis is a platform on AWS to send streaming data to, making it easy to load and analyse. Providing the ability to build custom apps.

Kinesis Streams

Kinesis Streams – data producers stream data to kinesis. Kinesis streams stores the data for 24hrs by default, up to 7 days possible. Data is contained in shards, typically a shard per data type. A shard can handle 5 transactions per second for read, up to 2MB/sec and up to 1000 records per second for writes up to 1MB per second including partition keys. The data capacity of the stream is a function of the number of shards specified in a stream, the total capacity of the stream is the sum of the capacities of its shards. EC2 can analyse shards and then store it in DynamoDB, S3, EMR, RDS or whatever. Kinesis streams allows persistent storage of stream data for 24hrs to 7 days.

Shards = Kinesis streams.

Kinesis Firehose

Kinesis Firehose – Producers send data streams to Kinesis Firehose. No persistent storage, data has to be processed immediately, usually by a lambda function which outputs to S3 and on to whatever.

Kinesis Analytics can analyse data on the fly from either streams or firehose, before passing output to S3, Redshift or Elastic Cluster.

Cognito

Web Identity Federation & Cognito. Access AWS resources after auth with web-based providers like Amazon, Facebook or Google. Cognito is the AWS service for this.

Cognito allows sign up and sign into apps, access for guests, brokers the identity transaction so you don't need to write the auth code, syncs data across multiple user devices. It is recommended for all mobile application AWS services.

The recommended approach is to have a user send an auth request to their chosen provider, be given an access token which is presented to Cognito, which then grants access to the AWS app.

Cognito provides temporary credentials that map to an IAM role, allowing access to the required resources. No need for apps to embed or store AWS credentials locally on the device and it gives users a seamless experience across devices.

Use pools are user directories used to manage sign up and sign in for mobile and web apps. Users can sign in directly to the userpool or using Facebook, amazon or google. Cognito acts as identity broker between the provider and AWS. Successful auth generates a JSON web token (JWT).

Identity pools provide temporary AWS credentials to access AWS services like S3 or DynamoDB.

Cognito tracks the association between user identity and the devices they sign in from. Push synchronisation is used to push updates and sync user data across multiple devices. Cognito uses SNS to send a notification to all the devices associated with a given user identity whenever data stored in the cloud changes.

User pools are user based for login etc. Identity pools authorise access to AWS resources.

Serverless

Lambda is a compute service where you upload code and create a function. Lambda will provision and manage servers for running the code and you don't have to interact with servers at all.

Lambda can be used as an event-driven compute service where Lambda runs code in response to events (triggers) – could be a change in an S3 bucket or DB table. It can also be used as a compute service to run code in response to HTTP requests using API gateway or API calls from AWS SDKs.

Always have API gateway at the front for serverless, then Lambda functions hitting a backend database (DynamoDB and Aurora Serverless are the serverless options), S3 bucket or other destination. Lambda will spool up an instance for every user independently on demand. 1:1 scaling – it scales out, not up.

Lambda supports Node.js, Java, Python, C#, Go & PowerShell.

Lambda priced per request, memory. First million are free, then $0.20 per million. Also billed on duration of request.

Lambda is great because there is no server, no need to manage them. Continuous scaling and super cheap.

Lambda, DynamoDB, Aurora Serverless, API gateway and S3 are Serverless.

Lambda functions can trigger other Lambda functions.

AWS A-ray allows you to debug serverless applications.

Lambda can do things globally, such as backup up S3 backups to other S3 buckets.

Know your triggers!

Lambda create functions – blueprints and application repository have loads of examples for Alexa skills you can build without knowing any code.

Good Luck!

The Exam when I took it had just been updated and featured 65 questions – most take the form of a couple of lines of scenario to set the scene, followed by a multiple-choice question.

It was a 2hr 10-minute exam, and I completed it in around 1hr 45mins. It was one of the more difficult associate level exams I have completed.

This book, plus the information I gathered studying AWS Technical Professional and Business Professional, and a decent familiarity with the AWS Console & CLI, were all I needed to pass Solutions Architect Associate and become an AWS Certified Solutions Architect!

Please keep in mind that although all the information in this book was accurate at the point of publication, cloud technologies evolve constantly. Check Amazon Whitepapers to ensure you have the most up to date information on the products and services offered by AWS.

Good Luck!

Contacting the Author

If you have any comments on this book, questions for me or suggestions for the next edition you can contact me at the following address:

publications@blackchili.co.uk.

You will find my professional profile on LinkedIn here:

https://www.linkedin.com/in/renhimself/